Which Way
to the Dragon!

Poems for the Coming-on-Strong

Which Way to the Dragon!

Poems for the Coming-on-Strong

Coming on Strong!
Sara Holbrook
6/97
Nashville, IN.

By Sara Holbrook

Boyds Mills Press

▲ ▲

To my niece and nephew,
Anne and Alan Meyer,
dragon slayers, both.

And to my sister Faun,
queen of their realm.

Published by Wordsong
Boyds Mills Press, Inc.
A Highlights Company
815 Church Street
Honesdale, Pennsylvania 18431
Printed in the United States of America

Publisher Cataloging-in-Publication Data
Holbrook, Sara.
    Which way to the dragon! : poems for the coming-on-strong / by Sara
Holbrook.—1st ed.
[48]p. ; cm.
Summary : Poems about problems and issues important to young people.
ISBN 1-56397-641-2
1. Youth—Attitudes—Juvenile Poetry. 2. Children's Poetry, American.
[1. Youth—Attitudes—Poetry. 2. American poetry.] I. Title.
811.54—dc20   1996   AC   CIP
Library of Congress Catalog Card Number 96-85176

First edition, 1996
Book designed by Tim Gillner
Cover concept and photography by The Reuben Group
The text of this book is set in 14-point Bodoni.

10 9 8 7 6 5 4 3 2

▼ ▼

TABLE OF CONTENTS

▲▲▲▲▲ ▲ ▲ ▲ ▲ ▲ ▲ ▲ ▲ ▲ ▲ ▲ ▲ ▲ ▲ ▲ ▲ ▲ ▲ ▲▲▲

▼ ▼

▲▲▲▲▲▲▲▲▲▲▲▲▲▲▲▲▲▲▲▲▲▲▲▲

▼▼▼▼▼▼▼▼▼▼▼▼▼▼▼▼▼▼▼▼▼▼▼▼

▲ ▲

WHICH WAY TO THE DRAGON!

I don't need a shield,
a helmet or lance,
I'm brave
and I'm bold—
dragons don't stand a chance.

My brain is my shield.
I stand my own guard.
My words are my lance.
My head is real hard.

I am armored with courage,
and I have the desire.
I'm short
but I'm quick.
I can even spit fire.

I'm sharper than steel
and I'm not just braggin'.
I'm coming on strong.
Which way to the dragon!

▲▲▲▲▲▲▲▲▲▲▲▲▲▲▲▲▲▲▲▲▲▲▲▲▲

MR. WHO

There is a ghost in our house,
we call him Mr. Who.
Who does all the things
a kid would never do.

Like put trays in the freezer
with no water or no ice.
Any kid would know
that wasn't very nice.

Who uses toilet paper
but doesn't change the roll,
eats cereal by the T.V.
and then steps in the bowl.

Who leaves his trucks and cars
spread out on the floor.
When Daddy walks in barefoot,
Who hides behind the door.

▼▼▼▼▼▼▼▼▼▼▼▼▼▼▼▼▼▼▼▼▼▼▼▼

Who won't take time to flush,
forgets to feed the cat,
always hides my shoes
and never puts milk back.

Who doesn't make the bed,
and when it's time for chores?
Who thinks it's kind of cute
to drag me out-of-doors.

And so I get in trouble.
What's a kid to do?
"Who did this?" they ask.
I shrug.
"Well, you know Who!"

WHAM-A-BAMA ONE-MAN BAND

I can stomp
like marching boots.
I can ringle-jingle
toot-a-hoot.
I can dum-ta-trum-dum
anything.
I can clatter, chatter
chink-a-ching.
I can clap-a-tap-a
railing sticks,
play my tummy,
play my lips.

I can cymbal-bimble
lids-a-pans,
howl like sirens,
clap my hands.

▲ ▲

I can buzz.
I can bam.
I can whistle.
I can slam.
If you listen
once to me,
there's no doubt
you will agree.

No one's
a louder sounder than
my wham-a-bama
one-man band.

▼ ▼

▲ ▲

COUNT DOWN

One for you,
two for me.
Counting candies,
one, two, three.

That's not fair?
You disagree?
One for you
and two for me?

Let's look again.
Now, let me see.
Wait!
Take them all.
They're sugar-free.

▼ ▼

▲ ▲

GRANDPA

It's fun to climb on Grandpa,
bounce and cuddle in.
But I have to spring
and squiggle
to avoid
THE CHIN.

With Grandpa's help
I might
become an acrobat
from scooping up his hugs
without a single scratch.

▲ ▲

THE TOOTH COMES OUT

The tooth comes out
with a little "ouch."
Now let me get this straight:
I put the tooth
in this envelope,
the fairy waits till late.
When I'm asleep
and you're asleep,
he sneaks in
like some robber creep,
steals my tooth
when he comes in
and scares me out of
all my skin?
Right.

He pays me for the tooth?

At first I thought,
"No way!"
But this might work okay.
How 'bout we lock the house
with double, triple locks.
Put this envelope
out in the mailbox.

And if this fairy's real
and with a little luck,
he'll find the tooth out there
and leave me a whole buck.

▲ ▲

THOUGHTS ABOUT THE BATH

Shampoo.
Boo hoo.

▼ ▼

▲ ▲

BUBBLES

Bubbles quiet squeakle sounds
when I get in the bath,
they open to make room for me
and then fill in the gaps.

I dress myself,
a suit of soft,
then dunk it down
and rinse it off.

I stick soap on
to form goatees
and build stiff peaks
on both my knees.

Bubble art drips off the tile.
I wash soap windows,
all the while,
I'm getting sad.
Suds always fade.
Still.
Think of all the fun they made.

▼ ▼

▲▲▲▲▲▲▲▲▲▲▲▲▲▲▲▲▲▲▲▲▲▲▲▲

NOT THAT MALL

Not that mall.
No way.
Not me.
That's no place
for a shopping spree.
I know that place,
it's filled with shirts,
and funny smells
and racks of skirts
and high-heeled shoes.
Stores that bore.
I just refuse.
I can't enjoy
ninety stores
and not one
toy to look at,
play with,
or adopt.

My motto is:
No toys,
no shop!

▼▼▼▼▼▼▼▼▼▼▼▼▼▼▼▼▼▼▼▼▼▼▼▼

▲ ▲

THE WORST

Wait and walk and wait.
Hunt and pay and bag.
Up/down piled-high aisles,
the grocery is a drag.

I'm still a carton too short to push,
a cookie too tall to ride.
I just go shopping for a place
to run and skip and hide.

The worst is not
the shivers from the freezers
or the fifteen miles of walking.
The worst
is carts getting double parked
and standing still
for grown-ups talking.

▲ ▲

A DANCER

A dancer
is what I will be.
I watch them on T.V.
I spin and dip with arms stretched wide,
and leave the ground so high a leap,
my flying feet are out of reach.
I make no sounds
when I touch down.
I float, I flutter,
I bow to the ground.

The music is what takes me up,
in slow, in sweeping strokes,
until it's fast and red and wild,
then I jump-snap-kick.
I'm faster than a drummer
beating with six sticks.

I practice everyday in my living room.
Surely someday soon,
the dancers on T.V.,
they really will be me.

▼ ▼

THE TRIP TO THE ZOO

The trip to the zoo
was crummy, because
the reindeer were home
but not Santa Claus.

I found a pine cone,
a pretty good stick,
fences to climb,
and railings to lick.

But then just about
got smothered by stink,
and I walked for a year
to get something to drink.

If you go to the zoo
take plenty of hours,
but don't touch the toilets
or pick any flowers.

THIS LOVE AND THAT

I've noticed there's a difference
between this love and that.
I really love my mother.
I really love my cat.

Some feelings are called love,
though they don't feel the same.
I guess because like everything,
they have to have a name.

Love acts at the movies,
love talks on T.V.
My favorite kind of love,
feels warm inside of me.

It hugs me when I'm hopeless
and won't leave me alone.
When I give a piece away,
it always comes back home.

▲ ▲

CLOSE CALL

I saw it all.
Bird walk.
Cat stalk.
Pounce.
Squawk.
Close call.

COPYCAT

I'm serious.	*I'm serious.*
Don't copy me.	*Don't copy me.*
I mean it, now.	*I mean it, now.*
You let me be.	*You let me be.*
I'm outta here.	*I'm outta here.*
Don't follow me.	*Don't follow me.*
I'm warning you.	*I'm warning you.*
Stop.	*Stop.*
Stop.	*Stop.*
STOP.	*Stop that.*
Stop that.	*No fair.*
No fair.	*You better quit!*
You started it!	

Geez.

▲ ▲

STAY!

Spider.
Spider.
Don't be a chump.
Stay on your web
while I pass . . .

PLEASE DON'T JUMP!

You may have eight legs
and I only have two,
but I'm pretty quick
with a step
and a shoe!

Stay stuck where you are
and stay out of my hair.
Me over here
and you over there.

▼ ▼

▲ ▲

MRS. GADD

Mrs. Gadd is practical.
Mrs. Gadd ain't sweet.
Mrs. Gadd once showed us kids
squirrel squish in the street.

She took us right up next to it.
We saw it all . . .
real plain.
She made us look and talk about
the way the squirrel
was rearranged.

I understand
the reason why,
to scare us
about cars.

▲ ▲

Of course when she was showing us
I found it kind of hard
not to be grossed out
or throw up on her shoes.
She told us to play in the yard
or we would turn to ooze.

She'd told us all that stuff before,
about cars going fast.
It wasn't the first time,
for sure.

Could be it was the last.

▲ ▲

THE LIGHTNING SHOW

The lightning show
is followed by
dramatic pause.

The clouds applaud.

▼ ▼

▲ ▲

LADYBUG

A ladybug
deliberately
climbed up
to sit on me.
It tickled me
so much,
I asked her
up to tea.

An ant came, too.
We didn't mind,
but ants,
we were to find,
even when
they're not invited,
never leave
their friends
behind.

▼ ▼

▲ ▲

PUPPY WITH POTENTIAL

This puppy
shows potential
for a promising career.
He seems to be a natural
puddle transfer
engineer.

▼ ▼

▲ ▲

JUST LOOKING

I went to the ocean,
just for a look,
and a grabby crab
took my whole foot.

He wrestled me
down to the shore
and pinned me to
the ocean floor.

Until about a
twelve-foot wave
performed a bold,
heroic save.

It snatched me from
the crab claw's reach
and slapped me safely
on the beach.

▼ ▼

▲ ▲

GETTING RIPPED OFF

Don't call me scared,
'cause I'm not afraid.
I just want to keep
this old Band-Aid.

If I ripped it off
it would be like undressing me.
Band-Aids are more than
a fashion accessory.

Why, it plugged up the spot
where I sprung out in leaks,
and dirty or not
it should stay there —
ten weeks.
AT LEAST!

We've become real close,
as you can see.
Epidermically speaking,
it's part of me.

▼ ▼

▲ ▲

MOVED

My friend Eddy moved.
It wasn't my fault.
They just packed him all up
with his dog
and took off.

With boxes and bikes
and leftover logs,
went his desk
and his chair,
and his *All About Frogs.*

A truck full of house
took Ed and his chairs
off to New York.

They left the stairs.

▼ ▼

▲ ▲

NO TASTE

The baby
has no taste.
Besides,
she is a dunce.
She pigged out
on the dog food.
Worse,
she did it
more than once.

▼ ▼

▲ ▲

JUMP-JACK-CRASH

Wiggle-klutz and Giggle-guts
like to spin
around.
They turn skip-tippy-tumbles,
gasp-crash-laughing down.

Up-jump spin
and down again,
ground-bound on
trippy toes
are
Wiggle-klutz and Giggle-guts
rock-rolling,
knees to nose.

▼ ▼

DOIN' TIME

I didn't push her down the stairs.
So tell me, is it just or fair?
I'm in my bedroom, doin' time.

A single, kind of dirty look
and an itty-bitty-bitty push.
Bang. In my bedroom, doin' time.

I didn't break my sister's neck.
You think for that I should catch heck?
Stuck in my bedroom, doin' time?

They told me that that kind of fall
could turn her to a vegetable.
So, I'm in my bedroom, doin' time.

I was thinking though, as off I went,
vegetable's an improvement.
Off to my bedroom, doin' time.

▲ ▲

"So what," is only what I said.
"She already is a cabbage head."
Slam. In my bedroom, doin' time.

I'll probably starve or even die
before I will apologize
from in my bedroom, doin' time.

I'll be found too late and just because
of the crippling push that never was.
Dead in my bedroom, doin' time.

▼ ▼

▲ ▲

SECRETS

If you'd tell me your problem
I'd tell you
I knew.
I'd give you a hug
and say,
"I'm worried, too."

Just because you haven't said,
it doesn't mean that I don't know.
Even though you act real private,
sometimes secrets show.

▲ ▲

THE GREATEST FUN

Soccer is the greatest fun.
I skinned my shin
and broke my thumb.
I tore my shirt,
my knees are bruised,
my feet both hurt,
my hand's abused,
my clothes are stained,
my head's a pain,
my ankle's sprained,
I'm spitting rain.
Forward or guard
it's just the same,
a low-down, grubby, grimy game
of rarely score
and kick and run.

Soccer is the greatest fun!

▼ ▼

HERE AND THERE

I can't wait till I get there.
I really hate to leave.
Here I have my hamster,
there, my friend named Steve.

What will Mom be doing
while I'm not here to watch?
I'm nervous she'll be lonely
or sit and cry a lot.

I can't wait to see my daddy
and huggle in his chair.
Sometimes we buy pizza.
I have my own room there.

Mom says she won't be lonely
just 'cause she's alone.
Maybe I'll send a postcard
or call her on the phone.

▲ ▲

My daddy says he needs me;
I brighten up his days.
We have to squeeze our sunshine
into weekend stays.

I think I have a headache
and I can't find my shoes.
It's time to go to Daddy's
and I've got transition blues.

▼ ▼

▲ ▲

I HATE GOOD-BYE

I said good-bye
to the beach this year
with a pocket of shells
and a little tear.

When my friend moved away,
I smiled good-bye,
then went to my room
for a private cry.

I hate good-bye.

It swells you up
then leaves you low.
Why does everything
have to go?

▼ ▼

When Molly went,
I curled on the floor,
like her,
in a heap.
I smelled the place
where she used to sleep.
And I swore on the day
that old dog died
that I had said
my last good-bye.

▲ ▲

EARACHE

There just is no pain
like an earache,
that comes in the middle of night,
when clock noises
come from the kitchen,
the hall glows with one yellow light.

I waken as if from a nightmare,
"That spider web's over my face!"
No.
Ow.
It's my ear.
Ouch. That hurts me.
"Mama," I cry out into space.
Mom comes
with warm drops
and the aspirin
and sits on the side of my bed.
She finds a cool place on the pillow
and smooths back the bangs on my head.

▼ ▼

▲ ▲

"There's roaring and rushing inside,
Mom.
Listen! Maybe you'll hear."
She comes close and smells like her
bathrobe
and says,
"No, it's just in your ear."

I cry, softly though,
it hurts badly.
Loud screams would just
make it ring.
I think having lived through an earache,
that I can survive
anything.

▼ ▼

IN MY CLOSET

That dragon
hiding in my closet
doesn't scare me much.
He mumbles
and stumbles,
watches
and such.
But,
he stays in his place,
most of the time.

I keep his secrets
and he keeps mine.

▲ ▲

OUT AT FIRST

I took a wrong turn 'round the bases.
I got hit in the face with the ball.
I whacked my shin with the bat,
but what I remember most of all . . .

Was not stepping up to home plate
with my kinder-short-stop body,
but panic grabbing me by the throat
when I got stuck in the port-a-potty.

T-ball teaches about coordination,
sportsmanship and more.
I learned to hold my fear and my nose
while jiggling that door.

My eyes would start to water
as I began to bang and shout.
I'd throw myself against that door
and yell in triumph,
"Yippee!

I'm out!"

▼ ▼

▲ ▲

TO BE

I am
you see.
I am
what's me.
I am
not done.
I am
to be.

▼ ▼